*You will receive power
when
the Holy Spirit comes on you;
and
you will be my witnesses.
Acts 1:8, NIV*

THE DYNAMIC DIFFERENCE

David Petts

Gospel Publishing House
Springfield, Missouri

02-0484

Contents

1 A New Dimension 7

2 The Power of the Spirit 14

3 Have You Received? 28

4 Only a Gateway 40

5 Changed Attitudes 50

Appendix 1 61

Appendix 2 63

1

A New Dimension

The long climb in the heat of the August sunshine had been tiring. We were unaccustomed to this kind of exercise and the cool water of the mountain stream was inviting to our aching feet. Sensibly, Graham, Michael, and Daphne sat down to rest. But it was my first visit to Switzerland and somehow I felt that we were wasting an opportunity. There was so much more to see.

Leaving the others to paddle their feet, Larry and I climbed higher; but half an hour later we too had had enough. As we looked at the others a few hundred feet below us, we realized that we had come up the hard way. To our right there was an easier way down. Gratefully, we turned to take it, when suddenly, as if from nowhere, a large rock came hurtling down the mountainside toward the stream. I was directly in its path!

As a fairly athletic 19-year-old I should have been able to jump clear with relative ease, but I was gripped with terror, unable to move. As a Christian I might have thought of praying, but my mind refused to function. In a second it would hit me. The end had surely come. What happened next I shall never forget. As if by a miracle the danger passed. When only about a yard away the rock seemed to strike a small protrusion in the ground. Changing direction, it crashed into the stream below, missing me by inches! The danger was over as quickly as it had come. I heaved a sigh of inexpressible relief.

"Wow! That was lucky!"

"Lucky, David?" said Larry who had been watching from a few yards away. "That wasn't luck. That rock *couldn't* have hit you. I was praying for you."

It was that simple statement of faith that started a process of inquiry which was to lead to an experience that has revolutionized my life. Of course, as a Christian, I had always believed in prayer. In fact, I knew that my very existence was the result of prayer.

When at the age of 16 I had told my parents that I felt God was calling me to the ministry, they told me something I had not known before. Sometime before I was born the doctors had told them they would never be able to have children of their own. And so my parents had prayed. They had prayed that God would give them a son and that he would grow up to be a preacher of the gospel. God had answered their prayers, for He had not only given them a son, but also had called him to the work of the ministry.

Yes, I believed in prayer. But somehow this was different. Could the inaudible prayer of a simple believer—"Lord, don't let it hit him!"—really have saved my life that afternoon on the Swiss mountainside? If that were so, this man moved in a dimension of Christianity that I knew little or nothing about.

Later during that holiday in Switzerland I questioned Larry to see if I could discover the basic difference between his Christian faith and mine. Although from different denominational backgrounds, I discovered that we had much in common. Doctrinally, our beliefs were almost identical. We believed the same Bible, preached the same gospel, and worshiped the same Saviour. We both knew what it meant to be a born-again Christian. We both could remember the day when we had turned from our sins and trusted in Jesus to save us. We had both been baptized as believers by immersion in water. Basically, we had very much in common.

And yet this man had something I didn't have. Something indefinable, but something very real—a dynamic difference! I asked him what it was. He started to talk about an experience he had received after his conversion—"being baptized in the Holy Spirit," he called it—when the Holy Spirit had come and filled him to overflowing. He had "spoken in tongues" and told me I could read about it in the Book of Acts. It was at this point, however, that my interest began to wane. I certainly wanted to experience more of God in my life, but as for "speaking in tongues," I frankly couldn't see the point of it. If "being baptized in the Spirit" meant I had to speak in tongues, I decided I'd better forget about it!

And so I did! On returning to England I dismissed the subject from my mind and would perhaps have ignored it forever had it not been for the remarkable series of events that took place the following summer. Eileen, my fiance, and I were sitting in the youth meeting at our church singing from a well-known chorus book, when I happened to notice a list of books advertised on the back cover, one of which was titled *The Full Blessing of Pentecost* by Andrew Murray. Immediately I concluded that this book must deal with the subject about which Larry had been talking last year in Switzerland, and I suggested that we should write for it. The following Saturday morning Eileen received a reply from the advertisers saying that the book was (then) no longer available.

A little disappointed, I returned home to my parents' house for lunch. The meal was not quite ready, so I went into the living room to wait. On entering, I, happened to notice a book lying on the piano and casually picked it up—*The Full Blessing of Pentecost* by Andrew Murray!

But how did it get there? No one, except Eileen, knew anything of my interest in the subject. My parents did not know where the book had come from. It is true that my father has always had a large collection of books, but if it was his, he certainly never read it and did not know that he possessed it. And anyway, why wasn't it in the bookcase? No one to this day has any idea how that book came to be there on the piano on the very day that I had thought it to be unobtainable! Immediately, I became excitedly interested, and after reading the book both Eileen and I began to pray fervently that we too might be "baptized in the Holy Spirit."

But nothing seemed to happen! We prayed and prayed. We reread the Book of Acts. We saw that what we were asking for was scriptural. But somehow the heavens were as brass. Larry lived miles away, and I didn't know if he could help us anyway. We were thirsty for God, but didn't know where to turn.

And then, one day, we swallowed our pride, and decided to find the nearest Pentecostal church and see if they could help us. (We didn't know much about it, except that it was the kind of church Larry went to.) It was several miles from where we lived and we were completely unknown to the minister and the members. We informed no one that we were coming, but simply arrived at 7:30 on Tuesday evening and slipped in at the back of a well-attended prayer meeting. As far as we knew, we had entered unobserved—but God knew we were there, and He had something to say to us.

It was our first experience of hearing the gift of tongues. I had read about it in the Book of Acts and in 1 Corinthians 14, but wondered if the gift could possibly be genuinely exercised today. But the manifestation of the gift we were hearing was both scriptural and beautiful. Three rather lengthy but distinct utterances in tongues were followed by three "interpretations." But the amazing thing was not the nature of the languages spoken, but the *content* of the interpretations. *God was speaking to us! Directly to us!* The interpretation was so specific that it could not possibly have referred to anyone else! We were overcome with awe. God had seen our need, spoken to our hearts, and encouraged us in our search.

One of the clearest things we were reminded of was our need to get up early in the morning and pray. We left that meeting determined more than ever to seek earnestly for the power of the Spirit in our lives. But like the disciples of old, our spirits were willing but our flesh was weak! We didn't get up early in the morning to pray, but we did return the following Tuesday to the prayer meeting at the Pentecostal church. Again the Lord graciously spoke to us, this time through the gift of prophecy: "Thou hast not fulfilled the commandment of Thy Lord. Thou hast not arisen early in the morning to pray . . . ."

And so, step by step, God was preparing our hearts,

and one day, quite suddenly, at another of those prayer meetings, we were both baptized in the Holy Spirit as hands were laid upon us. "Lord," I had said, "I want the Baptism, but I don't want tongues! Anything but tongues, Lord! But, Lord," I added, "if You really want me to speak in tongues, I will." And I did! For 45 minutes! And I have done so every day since.

My experience of the baptism in the Holy Spirit was on September 8, 1959, just 1 month before going to Brasenose College, Oxford, to read philosophy, politics, and economics. I have often thought that my faith might well have failed under the relentless onslaught of the agnostic professors of philosophy, had it not been for the fact that I had entered into a new dimension of the awareness of the presence of God through the infilling of the Holy Spirit.

The Christian Union at Oxford was in a healthy condition, doctrinally sound, and evangelistically active. Fellowship with Christians from other denominations was stimulating and encouraging. But there was something missing. Although politely interested in my newfound experience, most of the other Christians, probably quite understandably, felt that anyone who "spoke in tongues" must be viewed with a modicum of suspicion, to say the least.

Of the 300 or so Christians who regularly met together at the Saturday night Bible study, there seemed to be only four others who had received a similar experience. Realizing that the baptism in the Spirit, though wonderful in itself, is essentially only a gateway into the whole realm of the supernatural gifts of the Spirit, we met together each week for prayer. Constantly we prayed that God would pour out His Spirit and revive His church, and that Christians of all denominations would see the need for the power of the Spirit.

In those little prayer meetings, which proved to be the beginning of the Students' Pentecostal Fellowship in Great Britain, the gifts of tongues, interpretation, and prophecy were frequently exercised, and God graciously encouraged and strengthened us. On one such occasion early in 1960, one of the group gave a remarkable prophecy. God *would* pour out His Spirit. Multitudes of Christians from all denominations would be filled with the Spirit. Students and professors alike would receive the experience. We could hardly believe it. It seemed impossible. At that time the modern "charismatic movement" had not yet begun, and humanly speaking, no one could ever have believed that it would.

As some of us look back over the last decade or so, we marvel at the grace of God. What had seemed impossible has happened. God is fulfilling His promise. Literally millions of Christians have received the Spirit and have found a new release of power in their worship and witness. In the experience of this writer alone in pastoral ministry and student work in colleges and universities in Great Britain, the United States, and Europe, hundreds have experienced the blessing. For all this we thank God.

But the purpose of this book is not merely to describe an experience. That these things are happening is common knowledge, but the final criterion for the validity of any religious movement is whether its teachings and practice are in harmony with the Scriptures, and it is to show that this is so that the remaining chapters have been written.

2

The Power of the Spirit

The disciples who were gathered in the Upper Room on the Day of Pentecost were a privileged group of people. From the depths of despair that had surrounded the tragic events of the first Good Friday, they had known the unspeakable joy of seeing the risen Christ. They had spoken with Him, eaten with Him—even touched Him. There was now no doubt about His resurrection. Not only had the apostles seen Him on several occasions, but also over 500 disciples had seen Him at one time (1 Corinthians 15:6).

Yes, Christ was risen! But that was not all. He had ascended. He had led them out as far as Bethany and commanded them to preach repentance among all nations. He had told them to wait until they were endued with power from on high. They would receive this power when the Holy Spirit came upon them and they would be His witnesses to the uttermost parts of the earth (Luke 24:46-53; Acts 1:1-8). When He had finished speaking, while they were still looking at Him, He was taken up (v. 9). They *saw* Him go—into heaven (v. 11).

Yes, they were privileged people. They had seen the risen Christ. He had opened their understanding that they might understand the Scriptures (Luke 24:45).

They had seen Him ascend to God's right hand in heavenly places, far above all principality, power, might, and dominion (Ephesians 1:20, 21). But they had not yet *begun* to win converts. In fact, if anything, their numbers had decreased. Of the 500 who had seen the risen Christ, only 120 seem to have been present on the Day of Pentecost (Acts 1:15). It was not until "they were all filled with the Holy Spirit" (2:4) that things began to be different.

And what a difference there was! On the Day of Pentecost alone, 3000 were added to their number (v. 41), and more were added day by day (v. 47). Another 5000 came to Christ in Acts 4:4, and in 5:14 "multitudes" were added to the Lord. At a conservative estimate their numbers must have been between 8,000 and 10,000 people, but this number was to "multiply greatly" (6:7).

And so the Church grew. In some cases even whole communities turned to the Lord (9:35), or at least had the opportunity to do so (19:10). No wonder it was said of them that they had "turned the world upside down" (17:6). How did they do it? They had spent 3 years in the presence of Jesus. They had seen the risen Christ. He had opened their understanding of the Scriptures. They had seen Him ascend into heaven. But none of these things was the source of their power. The power came at Pentecost. Pentecost had been the turning point, for at Pentecost they had been filled with the Spirit.

But the power and fullness of the Holy Spirit was not just for those who had been present at Pentecost. All Christians were expected to be filled with the Spirit—and the command of Ephesians 5:18 holds good for Christians today. No Bible-believing Christian can dispute the need to be filled with the Spirit; but what is sometimes disputed is the nature of the infilling. The purpose of this chapter is to answer the question: "What does it mean to be filled with the Spirit?" To do so we must examine the nature, evidence, and purpose of the experience.

Its Nature

Close examination of the Book of Acts will reveal that a man who is filled with the Spirit receives a sudden, supernatural experience, subsequent to his conversion. That the experience is sudden is made clear in the first few verses of Acts 2. For 10 days the disciples had been awaiting the descent of the promised Holy Spirit. They were no more filled with the Spirit on the 9th day than they had been on the 1st day of waiting, but on the 10th day, when the Day of Pentecost was fully come, "*Suddenly* they were all filled with the Holy Ghost" (vv. 2, 4).

Similarly in 4:31, when the *same disciples* were filled again with the Holy Spirit, it is clear that the experience was sudden rather than gradual, for we read: "And when they had prayed, the place was shaken where they were assembled together; and they were all filled with the Holy Ghost, and they spake the word of God with boldness." In both these verses the Greek verb is in the aorist tense which is "strictly the expression of a *momentary* or *transient, single* action" (*Analytical Greek Lexicon*, Bagster).

That the infilling of the Holy Spirit is a sudden experience is further made clear in Acts 1:5 where Jesus promised the disciples that their infilling would be a "baptism" in the Holy Spirit. He likened the infilling, or baptism in the Spirit, to John's baptism with water; and whereas the mode of baptism today may be disputed among the churches, it is generally agreed that at least John's baptism was by total immersion. The consequences of making such a baptism *gradual* are obvious to all! Baptism is necessarily a sudden experience, and so by analogy is the baptism in the Holy Spirit.

Further, the apostle Peter, recounting the experience of Cornelius, declares: "And as I began to speak, the Holy Ghost fell on them, as on us at the beginning" (Acts 11:15). Peter identifies the experience of these Gentile converts with that which he himself had received "at the beginning," and since the disciples were "filled" at the beginning (2:4), it follows that Cornelius and his household were also "filled" with the Spirit.* And the expression Peter uses—"the Holy Spirit *fell on* them"—indicates yet again the sudden nature of this experience.

The importance of understanding that to be filled with the Spirit is to receive a sudden experience will be realized when it is remembered that traditionally some Christians have sincerely but erroneously identified the infilling of the Spirit with the gradual process of sanctification in the life of the believer. However, *nowhere* in the Scriptures is it suggested that the infilling of the Spirit is a gradual experience. On the contrary, as we have shown, it was always *sudden.*

But the infilling of the Spirit is also *supernatural.* Its purpose, effects, and evidence are supernatural. It is supernatural in essence. When a believer is filled with the Spirit, God, the Third Person of the Trinity

---

*The Scriptures use a variety of interchangeable expressions to refer to the baptism in the Holy Spirit. (See Appendix 1.)

who moved upon the face of the waters at Creation (Genesis 1:2), fills his mortal body. The Creator fills the creature with himself. This is completely beyond the normal experience of mortal man. This is supernatural!

In Biblical times when men and women were filled with the Spirit, they saw supernatural tongues of fire, heard the supernatural wind of the Spirit, and spoke by supernatural power in languages they had never learned (Acts 2); and a building was supernaturally shaken (Acts 4). Their prayer and their preaching were supernatural. They received supernatural guidance, power, protection, and even, apparently, supernatural transport! (Acts 8:39).

Only men supernaturally filled with God could see the results they saw, and if Christians today would, like them, "turn the world upside down," they too must be supernaturally filled with the Spirit. But this is something we must examine more closely when we consider the evidence of the fullness of the Holy Spirit.

If it is clear from the Scriptures that the infilling of the Spirit is a sudden and supernatural experience, it is equally clear that it is received *subsequent* to conversion. The disciples who were filled with the Spirit on the Day of Pentecost had left all to follow Jesus (Matthew 19:27). They had confessed that He was "the Christ, the Son of the living God" (Matthew 16:16). He had pronounced them clean (John 15:3). Their names were written in heaven (Luke 10:20). They were not only Christians (though that term had not yet been applied to them), but also cleansed, consecrated, confessing Christians, bound for heaven. It was not until the Day of Pentecost, however, that these disciples were "filled with the Holy Spirit." Their infilling was *subsequent* to their conversion.

The same was true of the Samaritan believers in Acts 8. They "gave heed" to the preaching of the Word (v. 6), and "they believed" and "were baptized, both men and women" (v. 12). When the apostles heard this, Peter and John were sent from Jerusalem to lay hands on the new converts "that they might receive the Holy Ghost: (for as yet he was fallen upon none of them: only they were baptized in the name of the Lord Jesus)" (vv. 14-16). There is no suggestion that the apostles were in any way dissatisfied with the Samaritans' conversion. On the contrary, they would never have laid hands upon them to receive the fullness of the Spirit if they had doubted their regeneration, for Jesus had clearly told them that "the world" could not receive the Spirit (John 14:17).

The phrase "fallen upon" (Acts 8:16) also occurs in 11:15, where it is used of the Spirit's filling Cornelius and his household. This implies that the Samaritans were also filled with the Spirit "as at the beginning." Moreover, the identity of the events at Samaria and Caesarea is clinched by the repetition on both occasions of the descriptive verb "to receive the Holy Ghost" (Acts 8:15, 17; 10:47).* These baptized believers at Samaria were, therefore, filled with the Spirit through the laying on of the apostles' hands, subsequent to their conversion.

A third example is the case of the Ephesian believers (Acts 19). Whatever their spiritual condition before Paul's visit we may be sure that Paul would never have baptized them in the name of the Lord

---

*See Appendix 1.

Jesus if they had not been born-again believers. It was after this that the apostle laid his hands upon them and "the Holy Ghost came on them; and they spake with tongues, and prophesied" (v. 6).

Now it is clear from these examples that this sudden, supernatural infilling of the Spirit was intended to be received as soon as possible after conversion. Indeed, in some cases, as in that of Cornelius' household (Acts 10:44-46), conversion and the infilling of the Spirit were almost simultaneous events. However, it is clear that there is a distinction between them, and that in all cases in Scripture the infilling of the Spirit is an experience *subsequent* to conversion.

Since, therefore, to be filled with the Spirit is to receive a sudden, supernatural experience subsequent to one's conversion, and since the Christian believer is *commanded* to be so filled (Ephesians 5:18), it is of the utmost importance that every Christian who has not received such an experience should avail himself of this blessed privilege at the earliest opportunity, possibly through the laying on of hands of a Spirit-filled believer.

Its Evidence

Unfortunately, there has been some disagreement among those who believe in the infilling of the Spirit as a sudden experience, subsequent to conversion, concerning the manifestation granted as an immediate evidence of that infilling. Some have suggested that there need not necessarily be any evidence. This view, however, is contrary to the whole emphasis of Scripture.

When Paul asked the Ephesians in Acts 19:2, "Have ye received the Holy Ghost since ye believed?" he implied by his very question that they would know if they had been filled with the Spirit. There would have been evidence. When the apostles asked the Early Church to choose some deacons, they instructed them to choose "men full of the Holy Ghost" (Acts 6:3). There clearly must have been some evidence that these men had received the infilling of the Spirit, or the disciples would not have known whom to choose!

Others agree that there is evidence of the infilling of the Spirit but suggest that it is to be found in the changed life of the Spirit-filled believer. Of course, the believer's life *is* changed by the infilling of the Spirit, but as has already been shown, in the Book of Acts amazing *supernatural* manifestations invariably took place both at the time of and after the infilling.

Others assert that the Church today cannot expect manifestations similar to those experienced by the Early Church. They insist that it is dangerous to derive doctrine from the Book of Acts. Yet in 2 Timothy 3:16 we read, "All Scripture is . . . profitable for doctrine." This means that as a part of the canon of Holy Scripture the Book of Acts *is* profitable for doctrine; and if this means anything at all, it means that the Church should work on the same principles *now* as it did *then*, and it should pray for and expect the same manifestations and results today as it experienced then.

Similarly, the evidence by which we recognize today that a believer has been filled with the Spirit should be the same as the Early Church recognized. Examination of the relevant Scripture passages shows us that this immediate initial evidence is "speaking with tongues." Although there are passages relating to the infilling of the Spirit where speaking in tongues is not mentioned, nevertheless, in all cases where an evidence of the infilling of the Spirit is recorded, it is "tongues."

This is more clearly seen from the table below which lists the four incidents recorded in Acts to which we have already referred:

	Disciples Filled With the Spirit	*Number Concerned*	*Accompanying Supernatural Manifestations*
Acts 2:1-4	Those in the Upper Room	120	Tongues of fire. The sound of wind. All 120 speaking in tongues.
Acts 8:5-19	Samaritans	Unspecified	Manifestation not recorded
Acts 10:44-46	Cornelius' household	Unspecified	Speaking in tongues.
Acts 19:1-6	Ephesians	About 12	Speaking in tongues and prophesying.

It will be seen, therefore, that where the manifestations accompanying the infilling of the Spirit are recorded, the one recurring phenomenon is speaking with tongues. Moreover, on the one occasion where the manifestation granted by the Spirit is not recorded, there is strong evidence that it too was speaking with tongues. It is clear from Acts 8:18, 19 that Simon the Sorcerer *saw* something, and presumably a sorcerer would only part with his money in exchange for an ability more supernatural than that which he already possessed. He had already seen healings under Philip's ministry (vv. 6, 7) but what he saw now was clearly some other gift of the Spirit. It was almost certainly speaking with tongues: "It [tongues] was doubtless one of the visible manifestations among the earliest Samaritan believers" (*New Bible Dictionary*, I.V.F.).

It would be quite wrong, however, to conjecture that the Samaritans spoke with tongues when they were filled with the Spirit if the Book of Acts did not make it abundantly clear that this was the evidence expected by the Early Church. In Acts 10:44 we read how the Holy Spirit fell on Cornelius' household, and in the following verses how the Jews who came with Peter were astonished that the Gentiles had received the gift of the Spirit, "for they heard them speak with tongues."

Today there are millions of Christians all over the world who have not only received the Holy Spirit but *know* that they have, for they too have spoken with tongues and magnified God. Many who thought they had been filled with the Spirit but had not spoken in tongues have found upon subsequently doing so that their experience has been deepened and enriched, and they no longer doubt that they too have been filled with the Spirit "as at the beginning."

It is clear, therefore, that any "infilling" of the Holy Spirit that is not accompanied by speaking in tongues falls short of the normal scriptural pattern. Moreover (as will be clear when the purpose of the infilling of the Spirit is considered), the idea of a Spirit-filled believer who could not speak in tongues would render meaningless the terminology used by the apostle Paul in his epistles.

Its Purpose

The purpose for which God has poured out the gift of the Holy Spirit is of extreme importance to the Christian, since those who have not been filled with His Spirit are in danger of falling short of God's perfect will for their lives.

First, the believer is filled with the Spirit so he might worship God with his spirit. In Ephesians 5:18-20 we read: "Be filled with the Spirit; speaking to yourselves in psalms and hymns and spiritual songs, singing and making melody in your heart to the Lord; giving thanks always for all things unto God and the Father in the name of our Lord Jesus Christ." Here is a dimension of worship into which only the Spirit-filled believer can enter.

In 1 Corinthians 14:14, 15 we are told: "For if I pray in an unknown tongue, my spirit prayeth, but my understanding is unfruitful. What is it then? I will pray with the spirit, and I will pray with the understanding also: I will sing with the spirit, and I will sing with the understanding also." Here Paul defines the ability to speak and sing in tongues as the ability to pray and praise with the Spirit.

In writing to the Ephesians he exhorts them to be filled with the Spirit, speaking to themselves in "spiritual songs," songs "with the spirit," the very words and tune of which are not learned with the natural mind, but are Holy Spirit inspired. If there were such a person in the New Testament as a Spirit-filled believer who was unable to speak in tongues, such an exhortation would have very little meaning for him. So too would the command of Ephesians 6:18: "Praying always with all prayer and supplication in the Spirit." Since Paul says that tongues is a form of prayer, his command to pray with all prayer must surely include prayer with the Spirit, that is, in tongues.

Meaningless also to such a believer would be the exhortation in Jude 20 to build up himself in his most holy faith, praying in the Holy Spirit. Comparing this verse with 1 Corinthians 14:4 where we are told that "he that speaketh in an unknown tongue edifieth himself" (builds himself up), and 1 Corinthians 14:14 which tells us that tongues is prayer with the Spirit, we see that Jude is exhorting the believer to build himself up—edify himself—in his most holy faith, praying in the Holy Spirit, that is, with the Spirit, or in tongues.

It will be seen from these passages, then, that just as all believers are intended to be filled with the Spirit (Ephesians 5:18), so too they are all intended (as a result of that infilling) to be able to pray and praise "with the spirit" in an unknown tongue. Such is one of the glorious purposes of the infilling of the Spirit.*

The first purpose of the infilling of the Spirit, then, is that the believer might praise God fully; the second main purpose of the experience is that he might be equipped with power to witness for Christ. The first purpose is God-ward; the second purpose is man-ward.

In Acts 1:8 we read, "Ye shall receive power, after that the Holy Ghost is come upon you: and ye shall be witnesses unto me . . . unto the uttermost part of the earth." (Compare also Luke 24:46-49.) The infilling of the Spirit not only helps the believer to show

---

*See Appendix 2: "Do All Speak With Tongues?"

his love for God in Spirit-anointed praise and prayer but also enables him to demonstrate his love for his fellowmen as his Spirit-directed testimony points them to Christ.

Peter, who was filled with the Spirit in Acts 2, was immediately instrumental in bringing 3000 to Christ. Filled again in 4:8, he was enabled to answer boldly the accusing rulers of the Jews. In verse 31, he received (along with the rest of the church) yet another infilling of the Spirit, that he might speak the Word of God with boldness. Few would deny that this is the pressing need in the Church today.

Finally, the purpose of the infilling of the Spirit is to satisfy the Christian. The fullness is directed not only upward to God and outward to men, but also inward to the believer himself. God is glorified as He receives Spirit-anointed worship; the unbeliever is convicted as he listens to Spirit-empowered testimony pointing him to Christ; and, thank God, the believer himself is satisfied with all the fullness of God.

In John 7:37-39 Jesus cried: "If any man thirst, let him come unto me, and drink. He that believeth on me, as the Scripture hath said, out of his belly shall flow rivers of living water. (But this spake he of the Spirit, which they that believe on him should receive . . .)." There is within the heart of every consecrated Christian a desire to not only love and serve God better but also to possess more and more of God himself. He knows the experience of the Psalmist who cried, "As the hart panteth after the water brooks, so panteth my soul after thee, O God. My soul thirsteth for God, for the living God" (Psalm 42:1, 2).

Thank God that through this mighty soul-satisfying experience of the infilling of the Spirit, our Lord has provided the way whereby every believer might drink to his utmost satisfaction of all the fullness of the Spirit of God himself.

Insofar, therefore, as the Christian believer is commanded to "be filled with the Spirit," he is commanded to receive a sudden, supernatural experience subsequent to his conversion. As a result of this he will not only find himself able to speak in a language he has never learned, and thus pray "with the spirit" as well as "with the understanding," but he will also know the joy and privilege of Spirit-filled worship and praise to his Saviour, Spirit-anointed testimony to the sinner, and spiritual satisfaction in the depths of his soul.

To those who feel the challenge of these words and the need for a deeper spiritual experience, Jesus still says: "If any man thirst, let him come unto me and drink." "He filleth the hungry soul with goodness." "He pours floods upon the dry ground." "He satisfieth the longing soul." In the next chapter we shall consider how we may receive and maintain the fullness of the Spirit. If you are really sincere, God will not disappoint you.

3

Have You Received?

When the apostle Paul arrived in Ephesus, he asked the disciples he found there, "Have ye received the Holy Ghost since ye believed?" (Acts 19:2). The question not only implies that receiving the gift of the Holy Spirit is a clearly recognizable experience that follows conversion (as we saw in the last chapter), but also that the matter is one of extreme importance, for this was the very first question the apostle asked them.

The sense of urgency with which the Early Church viewed this subject is also seen in the attitude of the apostles at Jerusalem in Acts 8. As soon as they heard that Samaria had received the Word of God, they sent Peter and John to them that they might receive the Holy Spirit (vv. 14-16). When they had done this, they testified and preached the Word of the Lord (v. 25) and returned to Jerusalem. While the great importance of the apostles' preaching must never be underestimated, it is clear that the primary purpose of their visit was that the new converts at Samaria might receive the Holy Spirit.

The apostles were very much aware of the difference the power of the Holy Spirit had made in their own lives. Jesus himself had commanded them not to depart from Jerusalem, but to wait until they were endued with power from on high (Acts 1:4; Luke 24:49). And what was important for the apostles was important for their converts. They too needed the Holy Spirit's power that they might witness for their Saviour. The promise of the gift of the Holy Spirit extended not only to their converts, but also to their converts' converts, "to all that are afar off, even as many as the Lord our God shall call" (Acts 2:39). The gift of the Holy Spirit is the rightful inheritance of every true Christian. We will now seek to show from the Scriptures how the Gift may be received.

The Holy Spirit Is a Gift

First, it is extremely important to realize that the Holy Spirit is a gift. "The gift of the Holy Spirit" is referred to in Acts 2:38 and 10:45. Peter talks about the Holy Spirit "whom God hath given to them that obey him" (5:32), and again refers to the Holy Spirit as a gift in 8:20 and 11:17. Jesus himself told us that our Heavenly Father would give the Holy Spirit to those who ask Him (Luke 11:13). In this connection it will be helpful to notice three things.

The Gift Cannot Be Earned. Since the Holy Spirit is shown to be a gift, it follows quite logically that there is no way we can earn or pay for the right to receive Him. As Christians we know that we will never be worthy to enter heaven by virtue of our own goodness. Our certainty of eternal life depends not on our own righteousness, but on Christ's atoning work on the cross. We enter heaven because we are justified (made righteous) by faith. So, too, we shall never be worthy in our own strength to receive the fullness of the Holy Spirit. But God has washed us. God has justified us. He looks on us as though we had never sinned at all. That is what justification means. It is He who has fitted us for heaven, and it is because of His redeeming grace that we may receive (not earn or merit) a foretaste of heaven, the gift of the Holy Spirit.

The Gift Has Already Been Given. Some gifts have to be waited for. Others are simply there to be received. The child who has been promised a gift for Christmas must wait until December 25th. But when the day has come the waiting period is over. The gift is there to be taken.

Before the Day of Pentecost the Holy Spirit was promised (Joel 2:28; Acts 1:4), but He was not yet given (John 7:39) for Jesus was not yet glorified. At Pentecost, however, the promise was fulfilled. The Holy Spirit was outpoured for all flesh to receive (Acts 2:17). The waiting period was over. The Gift was there to be taken, and after Pentecost we fail to find a single occasion when Christians waited or "tarried" for the gift of the Holy Spirit. Adjustments in our own attitudes and actions may be necessary, but from God's side there is no need for us to tarry—there is nothing further to wait for! The Gift has been given.

The Gift Must Be Received. In the Book of Acts we discover that after Pentecost those who were filled with the Spirit were young converts. They simply received the gift of the Holy Spirit.

Some time ago, before entering the full-time ministry, I spent several years as a schoolteacher while pastoring a small church in Colchester, England. Eventually, as the church grew and multiplied under the blessing of God, it became necessary to give up teaching. The staff of the school kindly decided to make a small presentation, and the assistant principal was appointed to inquire what kind of gift would be suitable. I told him I would like a Bible. Accordingly, the Bible was *promised.* The next day the assistant principal went out and bought the Bible I had been promised. And so the Bible was *purchased.* (It was mine already. It had been purchased for me. But I had not received it yet.)

Eventually the great day came! The principal said a few kind words, and the Bible was *presented.* But it was not until I came to the front, shook the principal's hand, and took the Bible from him, that I received the Bible as my own personal *possession.* The Bible had been promised, purchased, and presented. It was mine! But I did not *possess* it until I came and *received* it from the giver.

So, too, with the Holy Spirit. Promised by God through the prophet Joel (Joel 2:28), the Gift was purchased by the atoning death of Christ. (It was because He went away—the way of the cross—that Jesus could send the Holy Spirit (John 16:7).) At Pentecost the Gift was presented to the waiting Church, and ever since those who would possess the Gift have only needed to come and receive in simple faith.

Who May Receive the Gift

Although, as we have seen already, the Holy Spirit must be received as a gift and can in no way be earned or paid for by human merit, there are, nevertheless, certain conditions that must be fulfilled. Two important conditions indicated in the New Testament are repentance and thirst.

Repentance. The Bible tells us that God commands all men everywhere to repent (Acts 17:30). John preached the baptism of repentance for the remission of sins (Mark 1:4) and Jesus continued the message (v. 15). Those who would not repent, would perish (Luke 13:3, 5). Repentance is the first essential of the gospel, the first requirement for conversion. The apostles were commanded to preach repentance among all nations beginning at Jerusalem (Luke 24:47).

On the Day of Pentecost, when the cosmopolitan crowd, convicted by the powerful preaching of the apostle Peter, asked, "Men and brethren, what shall we do?" Peter replied, "Repent, and be baptized every one of you in the name of Jesus Christ for the remission of sins, and ye shall receive the gift of the Holy Ghost" (Acts 2:38). Before a man can receive the Spirit, he must become a Christian. "The world" cannot receive Him (John 14:17).

To become a true Christian a man must repent. He must recognize his sin, be sorry for his sin, and turn from his sin. He must turn to Christ who alone can save him, and trust in the merits of His atoning death. The fullness of the Spirit is given to endue a man with power to witness for Christ, but if he himself has not repented of his sin and turned to Christ, he has no experience of which to testify.

One of the most saddening features of the recent increase in popular awareness of the moving of the Holy Spirit among the churches is that there have been those who have inquisitively sought the Spirit's power without ever having surrendered to the Spirit's conviction of the need for personal repentance and salvation. If we would receive the gift of the Holy Spirit, we must first repent and turn to Christ. Even

Christians would do well to remember that true repentance is expressed in altered actions, and the Holy Spirit is still given to "them that obey him" (Acts 5:32).

Thirst. The other condition indicated in the New Testament is thirst. Jesus said that once the Holy Spirit had been given, anyone who was thirsty might come to Him and drink (John 7:37-39). The man who is truly thirsty will drink. Once we have repented of our sins, trusted Christ to save us, and expressed our newfound faith by obedience to the Lord, the only condition that remains is thirst. If there is any waiting to be done, it is not because the Holy Spirit has not yet been outpoured but that we are not yet thirsty enough to drink.

It is not enough to be merely interested in the subject. It is not enough to wish that we too could speak in tongues. Our soul must pant for the living God. Our natural and material desires will pale into insignificance when we are truly thirsty for God himself. God imposes no limitation on the Gift He gives. The Spirit is given "without measure" (3:34, *NASB)*. The Holy Spirit is poured out. It is for us to drink, and the only limitations are those we impose upon ourselves. But if we are truly thirsty, Jesus still says, "Come unto me, and drink."

How We May Receive the Gift

How, then, may we drink? How do we receive the gift of the Spirit? Notice, first, that Jesus says, "Come unto me." It is He who baptizes with the Holy Spirit (Matthew 3:11; Mark 1:8; Luke 3:16; John 1:33), and if we would be filled with the Spirit it is to Him that we must come.

Come to Jesus for Cleansing. As we have already seen, we cannot earn the right to receive the Holy Spirit, but at the same time we could hardly expect the *Holy* Spirit to fill an unclean vessel. This does *not* mean we must strive to achieve a certain level of holiness before the Spirit will fill us. The baptism in the Spirit is not just for spiritual giants but for young converts too, for "babes" in Christ.

The holiness we require is far greater than that which we ourselves can achieve, for all our righteousness is as filthy rags. The holiness we require is that which Jesus alone can give—the cleansing that fits us for heaven itself, the cleansing we receive at conversion. When we trust Christ to save us, our sins are remitted, washed away, forgiven. We are justified, counted as righteous. God sees us as if we had never sinned. Of course, we do sin, even after conversion. But God has graciously provided the means for our cleansing. "If we confess our sins, he is faithful and just to forgive us our sins, and to cleanse us from all unrighteousness" (1 John 1:9).

If you are seeking the gift of the Holy Spirit, you will almost certainly be conscious of sin in your life. But Jesus will *cleanse* you from *all* unrighteousness, if you will come to Him in repentance and confess your sin. Claim the promise of this verse and accept the cleansing He so freely offers.

Come to Jesus Expecting. Once we have come to Jesus for cleansing, we may come to Him expecting. We may expect Him to grant our request. "If our heart condemn us not, then have we confidence toward God. And whatsoever we ask, we receive of him" (1 John 3:21, 22).

In this connection, the passage in Luke 11:11-13 is

extremely significant. In verse 13 the Holy Spirit is promised to those who ask their Heavenly Father. (This cannot possibly refer to the work of the Holy Spirit at conversion, as those asking for the Holy Spirit are already sons.)

The passage teaches two main truths: first, that if we ask for the Holy Spirit, God will give us the Holy Spirit; and second, that when, as sons of God, we ask for the Holy Spirit, God will not let us receive "stones," "scorpions," or "serpents." Earthly fathers do not give their children such things, and Jesus promises that neither will our Heavenly Father allow His sons to receive harmful, counterfeit, or satanic gifts. Our Father does not deal in demons! When His children ask Him for the Holy Spirit, it is the Holy Spirit He gives!

Let us then ask for the Holy Spirit and expect to receive Him. Let us also expect to speak in tongues. As we saw in the previous chapter, speaking in tongues is the evidence the Holy Spirit gives that He has come. That is not to say that we are to *seek* for tongues. (Too many are doing just that.) We are to seek for the Holy Spirit, and in doing so we will *expect* to speak in tongues. In this connection please notice that speaking in tongues is something *you* do. The Holy Spirit does not speak in tongues—you do. Paul says: "If *I* pray in an unknown tongue, *my* spirit prayeth . . . . If any man speak in an unknown tongue . . ." (1 Corinthians 14:14, 27).

Nowhere does the Bible refer to the Holy Spirit speaking in tongues. The Holy Spirit gives the "utterance" (Acts 2:4). He makes sure the right sounds are formed, so to speak. But it is *we* who speak in tongues, and it is as we begin in faith to praise God in this way that we begin to pray "with the Spirit," as distinct from "with the understanding." But how can we be sure that the Gift is genuine? Because our Heavenly Father simply does *not* give serpents, scorpions, or stones to His children.

Come to Jesus in Worship. The disciples who were filled with the Spirit on the Day of Pentecost had spent much time in prayer (Acts 1:14), but they had also spent time in worship (Luke 24:49-53). Jesus had told them the Holy Spirit would come, and it seems the disciples not only prayed for His coming, but also praised God that He would come. Jesus had said: "If I depart, I will send him unto you" (John 16:7). The source of the disciples' joy as they waited for the coming of the Holy Spirit was that Jesus *had* departed.

They had seen Him go. He had told them they would be baptized with the Holy Spirit "not many days hence" (Acts 1:5). They would receive power for witnessing when the Spirit came (v. 8). And then, "while they beheld, he was taken up" (v. 9). They saw Him go into heaven (v. 11).

They had never seen Him like this before! They had seen Him as a carpenter, a teacher, a miracle worker, even as the Messiah. They had come to see Him as "the Christ, the Son of the Living God," and, eventually, after His resurrection, as "Lord and God." But always God upon earth. Now their gaze was lifted heavenward, far above all principality, power, might, and dominion, and every name that is named not only in this world but also in that which is to come.

Christ is ascended; He is King, He is Lord, He is God. He reigns in heaven, He reigns on earth, and He is Sovereign and Maker of the universe. All things are by Him, through Him, for Him, and unto Him. He is before all things. By Him all things exist. He is the cosmic Christ not just Jesus of Nazareth. He is King of kings and Lord of lords! Hallelujah! What a Saviour! No wonder they worshiped!

Will *you* worship Him? Worship Him with your understanding, but worship Him "with the spirit" also. Begin by faith to utter those newfound words of praise upon your lips. As you begin to speak, the Spirit will give the utterance. Yes, come to Jesus. Come for cleansing. Come expecting. Come in worship and adoration. Jesus *is* glorified. The Spirit has been given. If you are thirsty, come and drink!

Maintaining the Gift

Finally, once we have received the Gift, the Bible makes it clear the responsibility for maintaining it is ours. The Ephesians who, after they had believed, were sealed with the Holy Spirit (Ephesians 1:13), were commanded to maintain the experience by being constantly filled with the Spirit (5:18).

God has graciously filled us with His Spirit, but it is our responsibility to maintain the fullness. There are three main ways we may do so.

Prayer. The disciples were first filled with the Spirit while praying (Acts 1:14; 2:1-4), and it was while they were praying that they were filled again (Acts 4:31). Our private prayer life is of utmost importance in this matter of maintaining the fullness of the Spirit. Now, however, we may not only pray "with the understanding" in our own native language, but also pray "with the spirit" in other tongues. Having spoken in tongues when initially filled with the Spirit, let us daily stir up the Gift, building ourselves up in our most holy faith, praying in the Holy Spirit (Jude

20). "What is it then? I will pray with the spirit [in tongues], and I will pray with the understanding also" (1 Corinthians 14:15).

Again we see that tongues is not something that happens to us; it is something we do. Just as we deliberately make time for prayer (with understanding) and for Bible study, we should deliberately stir up the Gift that is in us by speaking with tongues every day.

Worship. Worship, too, is important as we seek to maintain the fullness of the Spirit. Paul tells us to "be filled with the Spirit; speaking to yourselves in psalms and hymns and spiritual songs, singing and making melody in your heart to the Lord" (Ephesians 5:18, 19).

The fullness of the Spirit is maintained by worship, and it is sad that some Christians seem to give expression to worship only when in public. The Spirit-filled life, however, is filled with praise in private as well as public, and again the gift of tongues will help us here, for we may not only "pray with the spirit" but "sing with the spirit also." One function of speaking in tongues is to magnify God (Acts 10:46). As such, it is an invaluable aid to worship, especially when the greatness of God seems too much for our natural language to express. Christians should set aside not only a daily prayer time, but also a daily praise time! We do not always *feel* like praising God, but we are told to "bless the Lord at all times." Whatever our circumstances, God is always worthy of our worship.

Yielded Lives. Finally, God has filled us with the Spirit for a purpose. If we would maintain our experience we must be yielded to Him. He has filled us with the Spirit, not only that we might worship, but also that we might witness (Acts 1:8). The Holy Spirit will never force us to witness for Christ, but He will empower our witness when we do so. It is not surprising that some Christians fail to maintain the fullness of the Spirit when they fail to use the gift for the purpose for which it is given. Every true Christian should want to tell others about the Saviour, and the Holy Spirit gives us the power to do so. We do not always *feel* His power,* but if we will obey His commands, He will confirm our word and those who need Jesus will be enabled to find Him.

---

*It may be helpful to remember that the Bible actually says little about *feeling* the Spirit's power. Of course, we may be stirred emotionally, as when the disciples were filled with joy as well as with the Spirit (Acts 13:52). We may even experience powerful physical sensations when the Spirit comes upon us. The disciples appeared to be drunk on the Day of Pentecost (Acts 2:13; c.f. Ephesians 5:18).

However, any physical sensations we *may* experience when we are first filled with the Spirit will not necessarily accompany subsequent infillings. When seeking to receive or to maintain the fullness of the Spirit, we should not look or wait for physical or emotional feelings. These may very well come; but the Spirit is essentially received by *faith* and not by feelings. We know that He has come, not by "tingles," but by *tongues*.

4
Only
a
Gateway

Once we have received the baptism in the Holy Spirit we must guard against the danger of feeling that we have "arrived." Although a wonderful experience in itself, the fullness of the Spirit is not essentially a goal but a gateway. Through it we enter into an entirely new realm—the realm of the supernatural. It is God's will for us that, having spoken in tongues, we should go on to possess other gifts of the Spirit.

In 1 Corinthians 12:1 we read, "Now concerning spiritual gifts, brethren, I would not have you ignorant." It is one of the tragedies of Church history that despite God's revealed will in this matter, millions of Christians have been kept in ignorance of this extremely important subject.

It would not be possible within the scope of this small book to deal in detail with each of the nine gifts of the Spirit listed in 1 Corinthians 12:4-11, but in this chapter we will outline what the Scriptures teach concerning the gifts of the Spirit as a whole. We will not only examine their nature, origin, and purpose, but also attempt to discover how we may receive them.

The Nature of the Gifts

They Are Gifts. In 1 Corinthians 12:4 we are told

that there are "diversities of gifts, but the same Spirit." The Greek word used here is *charisma* (plural, *charismata)*, which comes from the root word *charis* meaning "grace." The emphasis is that these are gifts that God has given because of His grace.

The word *charisma* is not only used to refer to spiritual gifts, but also to refer to natural gifts (all of which come from God's grace), as in 1 Corinthians 7:7 and Romans 12:6-8 where the *charismata* Paul lists seem to be a mixture of spiritual gifts like prophecy and natural gifts such as cheerfulness. In Romans 6:23 the word is further used to refer to the "gift of God" which "is eternal life through Jesus Christ our Lord." Again the emphasis is that this is a gift God has given because of His grace, and like salvation the gifts of the Spirit cannot be earned by human merit but must be received in humble gratitude and dependence on the grace of God.

They Are Spiritual. The gifts listed in 1 Corinthians 12 are not only gifts *(charismata)*, they are also described as "spiritual" *(pneumatika)* (v. 1). This is what distinguishes them from the natural *charismata* mentioned elsewhere. These gifts are not natural; they are spiritual. Indeed, they are supernatural, as may be seen from the context of Hebrews 2:4 where we read of "signs and wonders... miracles, and gifts of the Holy Ghost."

This is very important when considering the nature of each of the nine gifts in particular. It is clear that since the gifts are supernatural, speaking in tongues cannot possibly refer to a natural linguistic ability, as some have suggested; neither have the gifts of healing anything to do with the medical profession, necessary though that profession may be. The gifts of the Spirit are, by definition, spiritual.

They Are Manifestations. In 1 Corinthians 12:7 the gifts are referred to as manifestations. The Greek word *phanerosis* which is used here literally means "a clear display, an outward evidencing of a latent principle." The suggestion is that the latent principle is none other than the person of the Holy Spirit within us. The gifts are the outward evidence of His presence and power. A man may speak in a language he has never learned, because the omniscient Spirit dwells within. He may work a miracle, for the Omnipotent fills his being.

The Origin of the Gifts

It should not be assumed, however, that all miraculous phenomena are attributable to the power of the Holy Spirit. Satan has his miracle workers too! As we read the opening verses of 1 Corinthians 12 it is clear that Paul is very anxious that his readers should be able to distinguish the genuine from the counterfeit, the divine from the demonic. He does not want them to be ignorant of these things (v. 1), and reminds them that before they became Christians they had been idol worshipers (v. 2). Those who sacrifice to idols, sacrifice to devils (1 Corinthians 10:19-21). Their previous contact with demon power had been very real, and so Paul warns them that "no man speaking by the Spirit of God calleth Jesus accursed: and . . . no man can say that Jesus is Lord, but by the Holy Ghost" (1 Corinthians 12:3).

Here we are given a clear means of testing the origin of a supernatural manifestation. Does the speaker acknowledge the lordship of Jesus? If he does not, he is not of God, for it is God's revealed will that "at the name of Jesus every knee should bow, of things in heaven, and things in earth, and things under the earth; and that every tongue should confess that Jesus Christ is Lord, to the glory of God the Father" (Philippians 2:10, 11). Those who refuse to acknowledge that lordship are not of God, however pleasant their personality, however plausible their arguments, and however powerful their miracles.

Spiritual realities are eternally valid, and the test Paul gave the Corinthians nearly 2,000 years ago is applicable today. A "Christian" spiritualist may pay lip service to Christ in the course of a conversation, but he will not, indeed cannot, say, "Jesus is Lord," while controlled by his spirit-guide in the course of a seance.

A further interesting difference between the "gifts" of spiritism and the gifts of the Holy Spirit is made clear in 1 Corinthians 12:4-11. Spiritualist mediums with a variety of "gifts" will acknowledge that they receive them from a variety of spirits. One familiar spirit will give the gifts of healing, another the gift of tongues, and yet another the gift of prophecy, and so on. If a medium possesses three gifts, he almost invariably receives them from three spirits! That is something quite different from the gifts listed in verses 4-11, however. All nine of these gifts are given by the *one, same* Holy Spirit. The expression "the same Spirit" occurs again and again in these verses.

Finally, before leaving the subject of the counterfeit, let it be clearly stated that no true Spirit-baptized Christian need fear that his gifts are demonic. Our Heavenly Father not only gives "the Holy Spirit" to those who ask Him (Luke 11:13), He also gives "good gifts" (Matthew 7:11). Devils tremble in the presence of Christ. They have nothing at all to do with Him (Mark 1:24). If Christ dwells in our hearts by faith, we have nothing to fear, for "greater is he that is in you, than he that is in the world" (1 John 4:4).

The Purpose of the Gifts

In 1 Corinthians 12:7 we are told that the gifts are given for our benefit, and a careful examination of the New Testament reveals that there are three main ways these benefits are experienced.

In Evangelism. When Jesus commanded His disciples to go into all the world and preach the gospel to every creature, He promised them in Mark 16:17, 18 that miraculous signs (including tongues and healings) would accompany the preaching of the Word. Mark 16:20 tells us that this in fact took place, and the Book of Acts continues the story with a catalog of miracles that confirmed the message of the early disciples. "God also bearing them witness, both with signs and wonders, and with divers miracles, and gifts of the Holy Ghost, according to his own will" (Hebrews 2:4).

Paul could talk of how God had used him "to make the Gentiles obedient, by word and deed, through mighty signs and wonders, by the power of the Spirit of God; so that from Jerusalem, and round about unto Illyricum, I have fully preached the gospel of Christ" (Romans 15:18, 19). Does this imply that the gospel is not "fully preached" unless attested to by signs from heaven? At all events it is right that every Spirit-filled believer should pray like the early disciples that God might stretch forth His hand to heal, that signs and wonders might be done in the name of Jesus, and that

God's servants might preach His Word with boldness (Acts 4:29-31).

In Establishment. All evangelism in the New Testament was in the context of the local church. It either originated from a local church or resulted in the formation of a local church. By the preaching of the gospel God calls men and women to himself. He calls them out from the world into His church. (The word *church*—Greek, *ekklesia*—means "called-out ones.") Insofar, then, as the gifts of the Spirit are of benefit in the work of evangelism, they are of benefit in the work of the church, for true evangelism establishes churches.

Paul had not yet visited the church at Rome when he wrote to the Christians there. The origin of that church is shrouded in mystery. No one knows how it came into being. Possibly the "strangers of Rome" (Acts 2:10) present on the Day of Pentecost took the message back with them. At all events we know from secular history that by the time Paul wrote his epistle the church was a large and important one.*

And yet, in Romans 1:11 Paul tells them, "I long to see you, that I may impart unto you some spiritual gift *[charisma pneumatikon]*, to the end ye may be established." What gift of the Spirit he intended to impart, or how he intended to impart it, we do not know, but whatever it was, the clear implication is that spiritual gifts are not only of value in the establishment of a local church, but also that without them a church is not truly established however large its congregation or long its history.

In Edification. The gifts then are of use in

---

*Tacitus Annals 15:44 refers to "an immense multitude."

evangelizing the unconverted and in the establishment of the local church. Once established, the church will need to be edified. Here too the gifts play their part. When the church comes together, whatever gifts are exercised, "Let all things be done unto edifying" (1 Corinthians 14:26). Indeed, the value of a gift is determined by the measure in which it edifies the church, for "greater is he that prophesieth than he that speaketh with tongues, except he interpret that the church might receive edifying" (1 Corinthians 14:5). Accordingly, if we are zealous for spiritual gifts we must seek to excel "to the edifying of the church" (v. 12).

How We May Receive the Gifts

Since the gifts of the Spirit are so important not only in evangelism but also in the establishment and edification of the church, it is essential that we understand how they may be received. In this connection it is vital to remember that our *only* source for faith and practice must always be the infallible Word of God.

A tremendous amount of harm may be done by listening to accounts of how others have received the baptism or gifts of the Holy Spirit if their experience in these matters is not compared with and verified by the Scriptures. As a simple example, someone with the gift of prophecy may tell us that when the Holy Spirit inspires him to prophesy, he sees the words he is to speak written out, as if on a chalkboard, before his eyes. Now it would be quite wrong to suggest that the gift of prophecy cannot be received in this way, but it would be equally wrong to imply that the gift is always imparted in such a manner. For some, it would seem, the gift comes not visually but audibly, while for others—probably the great majority—a strong impression is felt in the spirit that certain things need to be said to God's people. God seems to deal with different people in different ways, but He *always* acts in conformity with the Scriptures.

In discussing how we may receive the gifts of the Spirit, then, we may say no more than what the Scriptures say. Once we have said that, we must leave the matter entirely to Him who distributes the gifts to each man "severally as he will" (1 Corinthians 12:11). However, from the human viewpoint it will be helpful if we may learn from the Scriptures what our understanding, attitude, and actions should be.

Our Understanding. When seeking for the gifts of the Holy Spirit it is obviously important that we understand what we are asking for. We need to remember they are gifts that come as a result of God's grace. As such, we cannot earn the right to possess them, for they are given "according to His own will" (Hebrews 2:4). We should remember too that they are *spiritual* gifts that come from the Holy Spirit. If we wish to receive them it is appropriate that we seek to stay full of the Spirit. As we are full of Him, the Spirit will manifest himself through us in the ways that please Him.

We should also bear in mind the purpose for which the gifts are given, and so examine our motives, asking ourselves exactly why we wish to receive them. If we will remember that the gifts are spiritual manifestations of the Holy Spirit within us, given either for evangelism or for the establishment and edification of the church, we may expect Him to give us what, in His grace, He knows is best.

Our Attitude. Although we are told that the Spirit divides to each man "severally as He will" (1 Corinthians 12:11), divine sovereignty in no way precludes human responsibility. God commands us to covet the gifts (1 Corinthians 12:31). The gifts of the Spirit are not some "optional extra" for which we may pray if we happen to be interested! We are *commanded* to covet.

It is interesting that in the realm of the spiritual God commands us to do the very thing which in the realm of the natural He forbids. "Thou shalt not covet," reads the 10th commandment (Exodus 20:17). But the things we are forbidden to covet are natural, material things—our neighbor's house, wife, servant, or animals. Perhaps it is significant that spiritual gifts seem more prevalent today in those parts of the worldwide Church where materialism is least in evidence; and perhaps if those of us who live in more prosperous nations were to spend less time in pursuit of material gain and devote more of our attention to the things of the Spirit, we would see the revival we so desperately need.

We are to covet the gifts (1 Corinthians 12:31); desire them (1 Corinthians 14:1); be zealous for them (v. 12). Although translated differently in each of these verses, the Greek word used on each occasion is actually the same, and literally means to strive fervently after, to be a devoted adherent, a zealot. It seems that God expects us not only to be thirsty for the Spirit himself, but also for the gifts the Spirit gives.

Our Actions. The man who truly covets something will eventually do something about getting it. Is there anything we can do to receive the gifts of the Spirit? First, the Scriptures show us we may *pray*. First Corinthians 14:13 encourages those who have the gift of tongues to pray for the gift of interpretation, and although it is only one specific gift that is referred to here, it would seem that if prayer is sanctioned as a means of obtaining one of the gifts, it must also be appropriate to pray for the others.

Second, we must exercise *faith*. The gifts of tongues and healings, for example, are promised to "them that believe" (Mark 16:17, 18), and those who prophesy must do so "according to the proportion of faith" (Romans 12:6). We must not only ask for the gifts in prayer, but also we must *believe* that God will give them, remembering that "faith without works is dead" and that if we really believe we will act.

Finally, perhaps it should be pointed out that inasmuch as the gifts are given for the edification of the church, and as it would seem unlikely that any gift would be manifested in a church that denies their validity or underestimates their importance, if we are really sincere in our desire to progress in the realm of the gifts of the Spirit, we will see to it that we worship where the Spirit is not quenched.

5

Changed Attitudes

As we have already seen, when a Christian is filled with the Spirit for the first time, the first thing that happens is that he begins to praise God in a language he has never learned. He begins to "speak with tongues." This was the evidence accepted by the Early Church (Acts 10:44-46) and it is the evidence we should accept today. However, the difference between a Christian who has been baptized in the Holy Spirit and one who has not should not just be a matter of speaking with tongues. There are other changes the Holy Spirit brings about in our lives.

Our Attitude Toward the World

Jesus told His disciples in John 14:17 that "the world" cannot receive the Holy Spirit. As His disciples, they were "not of the world," but He had chosen them "out of the world" and the world hated them for it (John 15:19). In 1 John 2:15, 16 we are told that we must "love not the world, neither the things that are in the world," the things of the world being "the lust of the flesh, and the lust of the eyes, and the pride of life." True Christians are in the world, but not of it; and true discipleship involves self-denial and the bearing of one's cross (Matthew 16:24).

The "words of the flesh" and "the fruit of the Spirit" are contrary to one another (Galatians 5:16-23); and the Christian who is full of the Holy Spirit will of necessity hold the things of the world lightly. One of the most significant effects of the fullness of the Spirit in Acts 2 is that they "sold their possessions and goods, and parted them to all men, as every man had need" (v. 45). The subsequent infilling in 4:31 produced a similar effect, for none of them said that any of the things he possessed was his own (v. 32), and "as many as were possessors of lands or houses sold them . . . and distribution was made to every man according as he had need" (vv. 34, 35). The things of this world pass away (1 John 2:17), but the things of the Spirit are everlasting (Galatians 6:8).

The things that are seen are temporal. Unseen spiritual realities are eternal (2 Corinthians 4:18). We are to set our affection on things above, not on things on the earth (Colossians 3:2). Of course, the things of the world will still tempt us even after we have been baptized in the Spirit.

Even Jesus was tempted in this way. Baptized in the Spirit at His baptism in the Jordan (Luke 3:22), He was led by the Spirit into the wilderness (4:1). There He overcame the devil's temptations by using the "sword of the Spirit, which is the word of God" (Ephesians 6:17). To each temptation He replied, "It is written." So He returned "in the power of the Spirit" into Galilee (Luke 4:14).

Satan will certainly tempt us with the things of the world, just as he tempted the Saviour. Demas forsook the work of God because he loved "this present world" (2 Timothy 4:10). The temptation is always there, but if we are being filled with the Spirit daily the world will hold little attraction for us. If we walk in the Spirit we will not fulfill the lusts of the flesh (Galatians 5:16).

Our Attitude Toward the Word

One of the most amazing effects of the Baptism on me was a radically changed attitude to the Word of God. Although brought up in a church that acknowledged the authority of the Scriptures, as an inquiring teenager I had come to doubt much of the Bible's contents, and to the consternation of my pastor had frequently voiced these doubts in public.

But the baptism in the Spirit changed all that. Overnight I found myself believing the Book. Some of the intellectual problems were still there, but somehow they were no longer important. God was speaking through the sacred page. Of course, it is not at all surprising that this should happen. Jesus told His disciples, "When he, the Spirit of truth is come, he will guide you into all truth" (John 16:13). Jesus, the Word of God, is truth (John 17:17). If it is the Holy Spirit who has filled us, we will of necessity expect to hear His voice through the pages of the Book He himself inspired to be written (2 Timothy 3:16).

The Scriptures were not written by the will of man but by the moving of the Holy Spirit, and if we would understand them correctly we must not seek to interpret them in accordance with our own private ideas, but by the inspiration of the Holy Spirit himself (2 Peter 1:20, 21). As we do so, we may well discover that some of the doctrines and practices of our particular church tradition are out of harmony with the emphasis of Scripture. If this is so we may be sure that it is our man-made tradition and not the Word of God that is at fault, and we will possibly need humility and courage if we are to admit that some of the things we have believed for years have been error. But this is just the stand that God requires of us.

There is a very real danger that the Word of God be made of none effect through our traditions (Mark 7:13), and as Spirit-filled Christians we must be willing to submit ourselves, our doctrines, and our traditions to the searchlight of the Spirit of truth himself as He seeks to lead us into all the truth as it is contained in the Word of God.

Further, if we are to wield the sword of the Spirit effectively in the battle against temptation, we must learn that man does not live by bread alone, but by every word of God (Luke 4:4). The fullness of the Spirit should effect within us a right attitude toward the Word of God, but it is by the Word itself that we conquer temptation. Jesus was full of the Spirit as He entered the wilderness to be tempted by the devil (Luke 4:1), but He still needed the sword of the Spirit (the Word of God) to overcome temptation. Satan's tactics have always been to attempt to discredit God's Word (Genesis 3:1-5), but we are not ignorant of his devices, and like Jesus we will conquer if, like Him, we can answer, "It is written."

Our Attitude Toward Worship

But the fullness of the Spirit should not only effect a change in our attitude toward the world and the Word of God. Our attitude toward worship should be changed. It is a sad fact that the majority of Christians seem to find it difficult to worship. For many the daily time of private communion with God is taken up largely with prayer and reading the Bible—

and thank God for Christians who do that regularly
—but little time is spent in actual *worship*. It seems as
though people don't know where to begin!

On the public scene the situation is hardly better.
We profess to go to church to worship God, but for
many even the great hymns of praise and adoration
are little more than a ritual to be performed. How
different was the attitude of the Psalmist who cried,
"Bless the Lord, O my soul: and all that is within me,
bless his holy name" (Psalm 103:1)! "O come, let us
sing unto the Lord: let us make a joyful noise to the
rock of our salvation. Let us come before his presence
with thanksgiving, and make a joyful noise unto him
with psalms" (95:1, 2).

How different too was the attitude of the apostle
Paul: "Be filled with the Spirit; speaking to yourselves
in psalms and hymns and spiritual songs, singing and
making melody in your heart to the Lord" (Ephesians
5:18, 19). Nothing could keep him from praising. He
had learned in whatever condition he found himself
to be content. Even the darkness of the Philippian
dungeon could not silence him: "At midnight Paul
and Silas prayed, and sang praises unto God" (Acts
16:25).

It is the ministry of the Holy Spirit to point men to
Christ (John 16:13, 14), and when our attention is
turned to Jesus, we Christians worship! When the disciples were filled with the Holy Spirit and spoke in
other tongues on the Day of Pentecost, they were
speaking "the wonderful works of God" (Acts 2:11).
When Cornelius received the Holy Spirit he was
heard to speak in tongues "and magnify God" (Acts
10:46).

As we saw in chapter 2, one of the great purposes

of the fullness of the Spirit is that we might worship God more fully. We should worship God in private. A part of every day should be set aside so we might worship as well as pray. We are urged to present our bodies to God as "a living sacrifice, holy, acceptable unto God, which is [our] reasonable service" (Romans 12:1). The word *service* here is better translated "worship." The apostle is beseeching us to present ourselves to God in worship, because of His mercies to us. We are to offer the sacrifice of praise to God continually; that is, "the fruit of our lips, giving thanks to his name" (Hebrews 13:15).

He has done so much for us. We have so much to thank Him for. Let us make time each day to give Him the praise that is due to His name. Let us thank Him in our native tongue. Let us praise Him in other tongues. Let us sing. Let us worship. Let us rejoice. For "great is the Lord and greatly to be praised" (Psalm 48:1).

And what is true of our private praise should be true of our public worship. In these days of ecumenism, many are suggesting that the diverse forms of worship found among the churches are a good thing. It is good, they say, that each man should worship God in his own way. But, surely, if God is God, and worth worshiping at all, we should be worshiping Him in His way!

Few have realized that the New Testament has set a pattern for us for public worship. There is no rigid order of service, it is true. But the general principles are given. God has told us how He would have us worship Him! "How is it then, brethren? when ye come together, every one of you hath a psalm, hath a doctrine, hath a tongue, hath a revelation, hath an interpretation. Let all things be done unto edifying" (1 Corinthians 14:26). This verse summarizes the principles of public worship, the details of which are worked out more fully in the chapter as a whole.

The first principle is *participation.* "Every one of you" is to take part. Every believer is involved. We all have a part to play. There is little room for a "one-man ministry" here. Second, there is *variety.* Not just psalms; not just doctrine; not just tongues. The Holy Spirit moves in a variety of ways (though never outside the scope of Scripture), and we must be subject to His moving. Notice the different types of manifestation to be expected. There is praise (a psalm). There is teaching (a doctrine). There is revelation (tongues and interpretation). The supernatural is in evidence. These things are not the exception but the norm.

If we are filled with the Spirit as individuals, we should be filled with the Spirit as a church. The gifts of the Spirit are not merely for our private use—not even for a private or semiprivate prayer meeting—but for the public life of the church. And if we would go on in the realm of the gifts of the Spirit, we will worship where the gifts are in evidence.

Last, there is *edification.* "Let all things be done unto edifying." Love is the great motivating factor behind all that we do (1 Corinthians 13). If we love our fellow worshipers we will want them to be edified. Our actions in public worship are to be determined by this principle. We should covet to prophesy, for this edifies the church (1 Corinthians 14:4). If we speak in tongues, we should pray for the gift of interpretation, that the church may be edified (v. 5). "Seek that ye may excel to the edifying of the church" (v. 12). "Let all things be done unto edifying" (v. 26).

These are the basic principles God prescribes for public worship—participation by every believer, variety of manifestation, with everything done for edification. A man who is full of the Spirit will be full of praise. He will worship God in private. He will worship God in public. But wherever he worships, his praises will be transformed by the supernatural power of God the Holy Spirit.

Our Attitude Toward Witnessing

Finally, the baptism in the Holy Spirit should bring about a change in our attitude toward our witness for Christ. This was the last thing that Jesus told His disciples before He ascended. "Ye shall receive power, after that the Holy Ghost is come upon you: and ye shall be witnesses unto me . . . unto the uttermost part of the earth" (Acts 1:8).

As we study the Book of Acts we discover there are three prepositions that are related to the word *witness* in a very important way. These prepositions are *of*, *to*, and *after*.

We Should Be Witnesses of the Resurrection. It is interesting to notice that while the preaching of the Early Church was centered on the Cross—"We preach Christ crucified" (1 Corinthians 1:23)—their testimony was invariably related to the Resurrection. Men must be told that they are sinners and that Christ died for them. But they also need to know that He is alive today and able to meet their needs. Jesus Christ is the same, yesterday, today, and forever (Hebrews 13:8).

When a new apostle was to be appointed to replace

Judas Iscariot, Peter told the disciples that one must be ordained to be a witness of the Resurrection (Acts 1:22). To the crowd on the Day of Pentecost he declared, "This Jesus hath God raised up, whereof we all are witnesses" (2:32). It was the same message to the Jewish council: "The God of our fathers raised up Jesus, whom ye slew. . . . And we are his witnesses of these things: (5:30, 32). And in 4:33 we read: "And with great power gave the apostles witness of the resurrection of the Lord Jesus." In the synagogue at Antioch Paul preached that Christ had died, "but God raised him from the dead: and he was seen many days of them which came up with him from Galilee to Jerusalem, who are his witnesses unto the people" (Acts 13:30, 31).

Shortly after he had seen the risen Christ, Paul was told: "Thou shalt be his witness unto all men of what thou hast seen and heard" (22:15). "I have appeared unto thee for this purpose, to make thee a minister and a witness both of these things which thou hast seen [the risen Christ], and of those things in the which I will appear unto thee" (26:16). From this last verse it is clear that the witness of the Early Church was not just to the objective fact of the Resurrection—the empty tomb, the Resurrection appearances —but to the fact that Christ continues to "appear" to His people. He is a daily, living reality in our lives. The Holy Spirit points us to Christ. As we worship Him daily He is real to us. We know He is alive. We too can be witnesses of His resurrection.

We Should Be Witnesses to All Men. The resurrection of Jesus Christ from the dead is such a glorious and momentous event in world history that God would have all men know of it. "Thou shalt be his witness unto all men" (Acts 22:15). But what does this mean? All nationalities? Yes, for we are to be witnesses in Jerusalem, Judea, Samaria, ". . . unto the uttermost part of the earth" (1:8). We are to teach all nations (Matthew 28:19). The gospel must be preached to every creature (Mark 16:15). But not just to all nationalities. We must witness to all classes of people.

Before Agrippa, Paul could say that he had witnessed "both to small and great" (Acts 26:22). None is excluded, whether it be the slave Onesimus, King Agrippa, or Caesar himself. All must hear the good news. All must know that Christ is risen! Our experience of the living Christ is not given to us that we might selfishly enjoy it in private, but that we might gladly share it with others. Not all will accept the message, but all must be told. Paul preached Christ, "warning every man, and teaching every man in all wisdom; that we may present every man perfect in Christ Jesus" (Colossians 1:28).

What an objective! If we are filled with the Spirit, let us see to it that we use the power God has given us for the purpose for which it was given.

We Should Be Witnesses After the Holy Spirit Has Come Upon Us. We finish where we started. Our great need is the power of the Holy Spirit. If we have not yet received the enduement with power from on high, let us seek until we find. When the disciples were filled with the Spirit on the Day of Pentecost, 3,000 people came to Christ. When they were filled again in Acts 4:31, they were enabled to "[speak] the word of God with boldness."

If we have been baptized with the Spirit, we still need to be filled again and again. We need a constant enduement with power. The blessings of yesterday are not enough for today. We must keep being filled. It is possible for God to add to His Church daily (Acts 2:47), but He will do it through those who are being filled with His Spirit. The task of spreading the good news is for all. In Acts 8:4 we read that those who "were scattered abroad went everywhere preaching the word;" but in verse 1 we are told that they were *all* scattered abroad. In other words, they *all* went everywhere spreading the Word.

If this is not true of the Christian church today, it is because some are rejecting the clear scriptural teaching concerning the need to receive the fullness of the Holy Spirit. And others who have received have failed to face up to the responsibilities that accompany the Blessing. But by the grace of God we need not fail. Let us maintain the gift of God that is within us and go out and tell the world that Christ is risen.

Appendix 1

Other Expressions Used
For the Fullness of the Spirit

	Pentecost	Samaria	Caesarea (Cornelius)	Ephesus
Being baptized with the Holy Spirit.	Acts 1:5; 11:15, 16		Acts 11: 15, 16	
The Holy Spirit coming or falling on or upon. (The Greek word *epi* is found on all occasions.)	Acts 1:8: "come upon "you." 2:17: "upon all flesh." 11:15: "fell on them as on us."	Acts 8:16 "fallen upon."	Acts 10:44: "fell on." 11:15: "fell on."	Acts 19:6: "came on."
Receiving (the gift of) the Holy Ghost.	Acts 11:17: "the like gift." 2:38: "You shall receive the gift of the Holy Ghost."	Acts 8:15, 17, 19: "Receive the Holy Ghost." 8:18: "Holy Ghost given." 8:20: "the gift of God."	Acts 10:45: "gift of the Holy Ghost." 11:17: "the like gift."	Acts 19:2: "Have ye received the Holy Ghost?"

From the nature of the events described in these passages it is clear that these expressions cannot refer to the work of the Holy Spirit at conversion for the following reasons:

1. The Holy Spirit "comes upon" us to give us power for witnessing (Acts 1:8). This is quite distinct from the work of regeneration.

2. The gift of the Holy Spirit referred to here was often imparted through the laying on of hands (e.g., Acts 8:18). The laying on of hands has nothing to do with conversion, as such.

3. The manifestation of speaking with tongues accompanied the reception of the Holy Spirit on these occasions, and tongues is not essential to salvation.

4. With the exception of Cornelius, the Holy Spirit was received after water baptism. Conversion preceded baptism in the New Testament.

Appendix 2

Do All Speak With Tongues?

It may be objected that it is unscriptural to insist that speaking in tongues will *always* accompany the initial infilling of the Spirit on the grounds that in 1 Corinthians 12:30, Paul asks, "Do all speak with tongues?" clearly implying that all do not.

A careful examination of 1 Corinthians 14, however, will reveal that there are two distinct functions of speaking with tongues, one private and the other public. In verses 18 and 19 Paul tells us: "I thank my God, I speak with tongues more than ye all: yet in the church I had rather speak five words with my understanding, . . . than ten thousand words in an unknown tongue." It is clear from these and other verses that for private use, for prayer "with the spirit," Paul valued highly his ability to speak in tongues. In the church, however, his teaching ministry was of far greater importance as it was of greater blessing to others than his ability to speak in tongues. Nevertheless, he makes it clear that there is a place for tongues in the church, provided that the utterance is interpreted, so the church might receive edifying (cf. vv. 5, 13).

The two distinct functions of speaking with tongues, therefore, are *private*, as a form of prayer, not requiring interpretation since only God is the hearer; and *public*, as an utterance requiring interpretation since it is heard by the whole church which will remain unedified unless it is interpreted.

Moreover, examining the context of 1 Corinthians 12:29, 30 where Paul asks the question, "Do all speak with tongues?" it becomes clear that the apostle is referring to the ability to bring a public utterance in tongues requiring interpretation and not to the ability to speak in tongues privately as prayer "with the spirit," since all the other gifts he lists are essentially for use in the church and not in private.

This question, therefore, which merely implies that not all believers have the sanction to speak in tongues publicly, in no way conflicts with the scriptural teaching that all Spirit-filled believers will be able to pray "with the spirit" as distinct from "with the understanding," and that privately, at least, they will all speak with tongues.